SPLENDORS
OF
MOSCOW
AND ITS SURROUNDINGS

SPLENDORS
OF
MOSCOW
AND ITS SURROUNDINGS

Introduction by Marcel Girard
Text by Vladimir Chernov and Marcel Girard
Translated by James Hogarth
Photographs by Gérard Bertin

125 illustrations in four colours
8 illustrations in two colours
133 illustrations in monochrome

THE WORLD PUBLISHING COMPANY - CLEVELAND

PUBLISHER'S NOTE

We should like to express our particular gratitude to Mr Vladimir A. Ankudinov, President of the Directorate of Foreign Tourism attached to the Council of Ministers of the Soviet Union, for the friendly way in which he used the great authority of his office to give us every help and support.

We must also express our gratitude for the valuable assistance we received from Mesdames Raissa Dovchenko, Keeper of the Tretyakov Gallery, and D. S. Libmann, Keeper of the Gallery of Painting in the Pushkin Museum; from the staff of the Armoury in the Kremlin and the Borodino Panorama; and from the authorities responsible for Leninskie Gorki, Yasnaya Polyana, and the Ostankino, Arkhangelskoye and Kuskovo Palaces. Our gratitude is also due to the Very Reverend Archimandrite Platon, Deacon of the Monastery of the Trinity and St Sergius, Zagorsk, for the very friendly reception he gave us. And finally we must express our warmest thanks to Mrs Svetlana Baranovskaya for the tireless devotion which she put at the disposal of those concerned in the production of this book.

This work is the result of the closest collaboration with the Novosti Press Agency, and we should like to express our appreciation of the very great help they have given us.

INTRODUCTION

The best way to arrive in Moscow is by road. You have driven through the night from the Polish frontier; you have kept steadily on over the steppe, barely noticing the few sleeping villages; you have passed close to one or two larger towns bearing the names of battles, and have continued on your eastward course, as if driven restlessly onward to meet the rising sun; and then, in the dawn, you see the town emerging from the plain like a mirage against the whitening horizon.

As you approach the heart of the city you find yourself moving back through the centuries. A dozen miles from the centre you cross the official boundary of Moscow, the ring road which casts a wide girdle round the city with its dual carriageway — leaving ample space within, for our road still passes through fields and woods. The first suburban areas are an uneasy compound of the old scattered villages and the planned satellite towns of today; but soon the cottages are seen no longer, the last market gardens and fields disappear, and we enter the twentieth century.

The twentieth century, however, is not remarkable for the quality of the houses it builds. From London to Pekin the world is being covered with cubes of greyish or pinkish masonry, with rows of uniform windows and flat roofs bristling with television aerials. The new districts of Moscow are no exception to the rule; but at least the allotment of space here is less miserly, for the land of Russia is of vast extent and all of it is in the hands of the State. In summer the drab monotony of the buildings is relieved by millions of trees, huge areas of grass, flower-beds and fountains. In winter the massive blocks of flats seem to float on the snow, and the lines of the streets are dissolved in the pervasive mist.

A few miles farther on we have moved some years backward in time. More exactly, we are back in the years before 1953. In that historic year the outward appearance of the city, like other things in Russia, began to change. The buildings erected before 1953 were grandiose and ponderous structures designed to serve the prestige of the State and its leader. The brickwork was camouflaged in stucco or embellished with stone ornament. The façades of Greek temples, complete with columns and pediments, could be seen hanging in mid-air, clapped on to the structure at the fifteenth floor. The tallest buildings were finished off with superstructures in a kind of Gothic style, elaborate patterns of turrets, pinnacles and spires soaring high into the clouds: of this type is the tall spire of the University. The ring of the Sadovaya is punctuated with buildings of this kind; and the whole skyline of Moscow is now jagged with tall towers, forming new landmarks to replace the spires and belfries of the old churches which have been swallowed up and submerged in the growing bulk of the town. This colossal style may not be to everyone's taste, but we may safely rely on the age-old spirit of Russia: Russia, we may be sure, will absorb these extravagances, as she has absorbed in her history the follies of the Tsars and of many others.

The area between this first ring road and the next ring, nearer the centre, which is known as the "green boulevards", belongs to the nineteenth century, a period of ease and elegance which in Russia still harks back to the eighteenth century. The houses are on the right scale for human needs. Their graceful façades are decorated with restrained classical ornament in milky white stone, contrasting with the light ochre of the facing. Behind the houses we catch a glimpse of gardens embowered in verdure and gay with birds, in which old-fashioned flowers — lilies, phlox, fuchsias, hollyhocks, scabious and balsam — flourish in uncontrolled luxuriance. The silent "house-museums" preserve their rooms and furnishings in the exact state in which they were left by those endearing heavily bearded figures — anarchists and revolutionaries though they might be when the occasion arose — who were the glory of nineteenth century Russia: Herzen, Tolstoy, Chekhov, Dostoevsky, Scriabin, Kropotkin, Ostrovsky. In these streets we must drive slowly, respecting the silence and the pigeons. Our eye is caught by all sorts of attractive little corners, and we make a mental note that we must come back and explore them on foot.

But now we are approaching the River Moskva. We descend a slight slope, and suddenly there in front of us are the embankment and the bridge; then the Kremlin bursts upon us, with the blaze of all its golden domes, throwing us five centuries backward into the past.

"This is the Tartar Rome!" cried Madame de Staël from the top of Ivan the Great's bell tower. But as we look round the buildings in the Kremlin and the Kitay-Gorod, the old "Chinese" town which abuts it to the north, we see that there is nothing of such antiquity left; nor do we see anything that is particularly exotic or barbarous. The new Palace of Congresses, a sober contemporary building of glass and aluminium, is merely the latest of the contributions which successive generations have made to the total architectural effect. Throughout the centuries men have been building, demolishing and rebuilding in the Kremlin, for many different purposes and in many different styles: the only thing that has remained untouched is the line of the enclosing walls, in large red bricks with swallow-tail merlons, built at the end of the fifteenth century in imitation of the castle of the Sforzas. Catherine II, that eighteenth century rationalist, wanted to raze them to the ground; but she died before achieving this, and her only contribution to the architecture of the Kremlin is a single green dome above the chamber of a Duma which never met, over which the red flag with the Soviet star now flies.

Here the centuries are mingled and the imagination is led astray. The Great Palace in the style of the boyars, with the hanging keystones of the windows and its huge roof in the shape of an upturned ship, looks an old building if there ever was one; but it was built for Nicholas I by a German architect, in a conscious effort to revive the old Russian style. The austere structure of the Arsenal was erected to the orders of Peter the Great, in spite of his ban on the use of stone except at Petersburg; but he had to build it to tame the rebellious feudal lords. These eleven tiny gilded "heads", the little domes which crown a many-coloured roof behind the Palace of the Patriarchs, are all that is left of the famous "Terems" in which the early Romanovs concealed their wives and their treasure; but if we are admitted into the secret courtyards we discover a fine architectural façade, and dark staircases, and golden grilles, and vaulted chambers, and wall paintings alive with monsters.

In these buildings we see history unfolded before our eyes, receding into the infinite distance of the past. The Time of Troubles was still able to produce the tallest bell tower, which bears the name of Ivan the Great but was in fact built by Boris Godunov, and was rebuilt by Alexander after its destruction by Napoleon's troops. The sixteenth century contributed the graceful Florentine *palazzo* whose rusticated stones catch the sun in summer and the snow in winter; and above all it endowed the Kremlin with its churches — the Annunciation, the Dormition, the Archangel Cathedral — in which a typically Russian style created at Pskov and Novgorod and Vladimir was meticulously reproduced and developed by Italian master builders. The shade of Ivan the Terrible haunts Cathedral Square and the Red Porch, but the only physical remains of his reign are a tall throne in the Cathedral of the Dormition and his tomb, hidden behind the iconostasis in the Archangel Cathedral, where all the Tsars and Princes of Russia rest in their inviolate tombs, from Ivan I Kalita ("Moneybag") to Fyodor Alekseevich, Peter the Great's elder brother, who died young.

The ramparts of the Kremlin, too, take us back into a distant past. The circuit of the walls follows the exact line of the palisade erected in the middle of the twelfth century by Yury Dolgoruky, "Long Arms", as a defence against wild beasts and enemies. We know, therefore, that there was some kind of human settlement on this spot in those early days. The name of the last corner tower, the Borovitsky Gate, reminds us that there was once a *bor*, a pine-wood, here. And in recent years pines and birches have again been planted on the slopes of the Kremlin, as if to recall that all things can return to their beginning.

Red Square also bears witness to man's long adventure on this spot. Its large sandstone paving stones have seen the passage of many different reigns, of invasion and revolution. Twenty-five generations of soldiers, craftsmen, merchants, peasants and conspirators have walked this square, and often have shed their blood. Lying in his glass tomb, with his face and hands exposed and his eyes closed, Lenin seems to be meditating on the epic story of the people whom he led at last to fulfil their highest destiny.

Capital of Russia and of the Soviet Union; the heart of the country's life, giving out much and receiving much in return, and the nerve-centre of international Communism; a traditional focus of

European culture and the place of origin of Russia's adventures into space — Moscow continues its confident progress into the future. It is urged on by a two-way impulse, like the constant beating of a heart. The people of Moscow are introvert one moment, extravert the next: now their thoughts are centred on their history and on their ancient Kremlin, now they are extending far into the steppe in an efflorescence of new housing, new schools and new factories. Their faith in the future and their activity in the present are both founded on the consciousness of their great past.

Moscow thus steadily pursues her destiny as a great city. She lives and changes; she has her moments of strength, as she has her weaknesses and failings. Like a human being, she has her own dignity and pride, and will not yield herself to the first comer. You must win her over gradually, learn her ways, speak to her gently, listen to what she has to say. You must, in fact, love her as you would love a person; for Moscow *is* a person.

Marcel GIRARD

I MOSCOW IN BYGONE DAYS

Moscow is eight hundred years old—though for a European city that is no great age. Nevertheless Moscow is much concerned to show us the remains of her great past: she is proud of them, and looks after them with care. Her historical museums and her libraries are full of old albums and engravings. And the scenes they represent —Kitay-Gorod, the Kremlin, the palaces of the boyars, the old monasteries, the bridges, the squares and market-places—are brought to life also by the imaginative power of the historical painters.

We must begin with these things if we want to understand and appreciate the full meaning of Russia as it is expressed in her people. The Soviet citizens of the present day are in two minds when confronted with this evidence of their past; now moved, now embarrassed to recognise themselves in these bearded ancestors in their long gowns. But they very quickly resolve their difficulty with a laugh: *their* life is in the present.

1 *The Kitay-Gorod. Detail from an engraving in Meyerberg's Album of 1661. (Ph. Novosti).*

2 *The Dulo Tower, Simonov Monastery, Moscow. Engraving by E. Leonov. Lenin Library. (Ph. Novosti).*

3 *The Ambassadors' Courtyard, Glinka Street. Engraving from Meyerberg's Album. (Ph. Novosti).*

4 *General view of Moscow in 1661. Engraving from Meyerberg's Album. (Ph. Novosti).*

5 *General view of the Kremlin and Red Square in 1661. Engraving from Meyerberg's Album. (Ph. Novosti).*

6 *Prince holding court in the Kremlin. Miniature from a legal text of Ivan the Terrible's time. State Historical Museum. (Ph. Novosti).*

7 *Building of a bridge over the Moskva. Miniature from the Book of the Tsars. State Historical Museum. (Ph. Novosti).*

8 *The Great Cathedral of the Donskoy Monastery (1684–1689). Engraving. State Historical Museum. (Ph. Novosti).*

9 *A street near the Myasnitsky Gate in the 17th century. Painting by A. Vasnetsov, 1926. Museum of History and Reconstruction of Moscow. (Ph. Novosti).*

10 *The old mouth of the Neglinnaya River, now underground. Painting by A. Vasnetsov. Museum of History and Reconstruction of Moscow. (Ph. Novosti).*

11 *Boyars' palace of 16th century. Reconstruction by K. Lonialo. Museum of History and Reconstruction of Moscow. (Ph. Novosti).*

12 *Tverskaya Barrier, Moscow. End of 18th century. Water colour. State Historical Museum. (Photo Novosti).*

13 *Okhotny Ryad (Market): hucksters and hackney-coachmen. 19th century lithograph. Museum of History and Reconstruction of Moscow. (Ph. Novosti).*

14 *Market in Trubnaya Square: dogs for sale. Lithograph by M. Yarovoy. Museum of History and Reconstruction of Moscow. (Ph. Novosti).*

15 *Alexandrovsky Gardens. Engraving from a drawing by Charlemagne. Early 19th century. In the centre can be seen the old Cathedral of the Saviour, destroyed after the Revolution. On this site was constructed the Moskva swimming pool (cf. Plate 140). Museum of Architecture. (Ph. Novosti).*

16 *Mineral water factory, Moscow. First half of 19th century. Lithograph. Museum of History and Reconstruction of Moscow. (Ph. Novosti).*

17 *Voskresensky Gate, Moscow. Lithograph. Middle of 19th century. Museum of History and Reconstruction of Moscow. (Ph. Novosti).*

18 *Andreyevsky Monastery, Moscow. Lithograph. 1847. Museum of History and Reconstruction of Moscow. (Ph. Novosti).*

19 *Church of St Nicholas of the Great Cross, Glinka Street, built 1678, now destroyed. Lithograph of mid 19th century. Museum of History and Reconstruction of Moscow. (Ph. Novosti).*

20 *Bread-seller. Detail from Plate 13. (Ph. Novosti).*

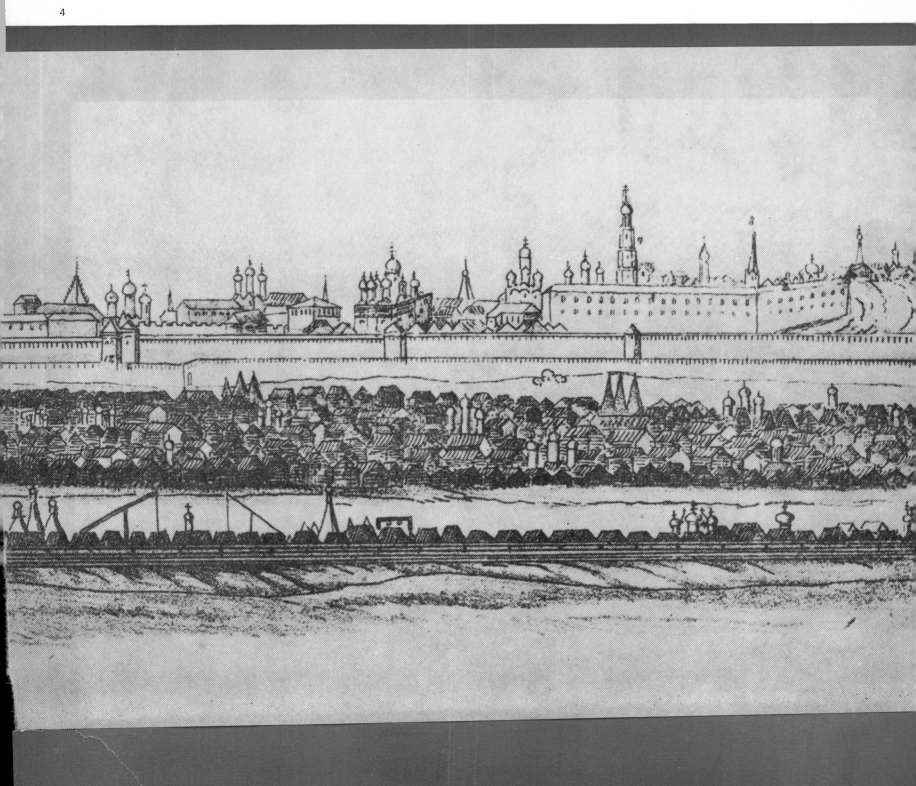

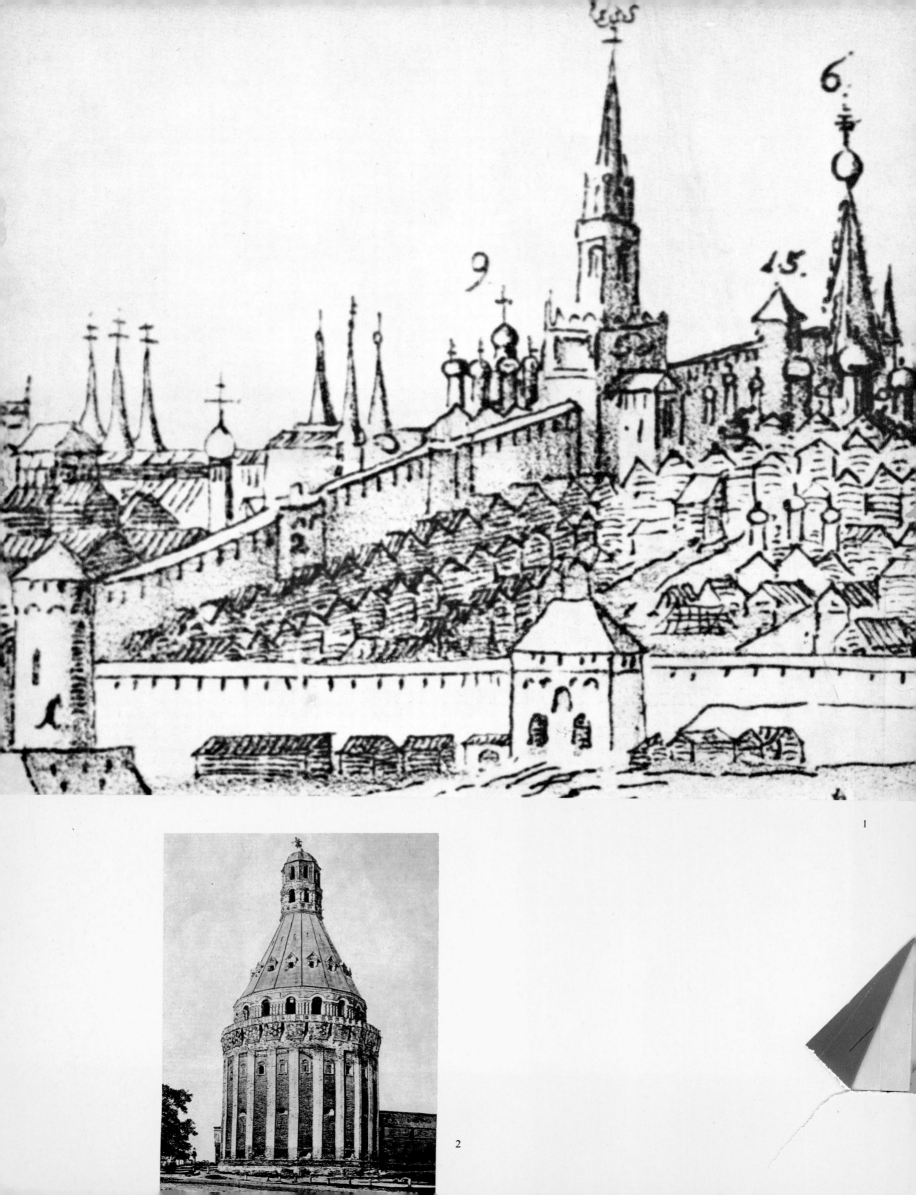

1

2

а братоусвоемоусны́ю юр̑гополасилїеонч
делатьцрь и великїпкнзьмвстошни
стити ницдорд да нседоегокняженїе
весон иоанонча дмитровоского по
зади иоана стоутопоссоколосолы .
ямихаиловесоcндорть юрге пнчазахарь
инла нныедворы делать снести ум̑
стошунстити пошграду помонасты
рсьбтмихаилоапчнда . ипозлубуlook̑

13

14

17

19, 20 →

18

II THE RIVER MOSKVA

The town and the river on which it stands have the same name—Moskva—and have been identified since the earliest days. Round the limpid water of this bend in the river, sheltered by a fold in the steppe, the first inhabitants, hunters and fishermen, found refuge. This tributary of a tributary of the Volga served them as a defence against brigands and wild beasts; as a means of passage through the forests both in summer and in winter; as a channel for the transport of goods from north and south; as a mirror to reflect the golden domes of their bell towers.

The Moskva is still at the centre of the city's existence, and new buildings—huge blocks of flats and offices, hotels, sports grounds, the University—stand at intervals along its banks. And to the young people of Moscow the river has always offered inexhaustible scope for the romantic reveries in which they delight.

24

25

III RED SQUARE

Since in Russian the words for "red" and "beautiful" have the same root, it may be that originally this area under the Kremlin was simply known as the "beautiful square".

Since then, however, so much blood has flowed over its old stones that we are more likely to call to mind the massacres by the Tatars, the Polish invasions, the executions, the battles, the civil wars and, in more recent times, the revolutions with which the square is associated.

Nowadays red becomes the dominant colour only on the evenings of lst May and 7th November, when the setting sun casts a blood-red glow over the brick walls of the Kremlin, and thousands of flags are carried in procession by the workers past the porphyry mausoleum in which Lenin lies at rest.

← 26, 27, 28

30

33

34

31

32

35

36, 37→

IV THE KREMLIN

In the eyes of Western historians the style of the Kremlin is not really Russian, any more than the name it bears in most European languages, an incorrect Polish transcription of the word *kreml*, meaning the castle, the acropolis, the citadel, the *burg*.

The enclosing wall with its swallow-tail merlons was imitated from an Italian model; the churches too were the work of "Fryazins" (Franks, Italians); Peter the Great's Arsenal and Catherine II's Senate House, with its green dome, are in the French classical style; the Great Palace was built by a German architect; and the new Palace of Congresses owes its ultra-modern lines to the use of glass and aluminium.

And yet the total effect is extraordinarily Russian. We feel this at once, seeing the golden outline of an onion-shaped dome against the sky, or the graceful silhouette of a birch-tree. Russian, too, are those fabulous jewels which once belonged to the Tsars, though they were made by Fabergé, or those coaches which seem at first sight works of barbaric splendour but yet were decorated by François Boucher.

Then when night falls the ruby-red stars which blaze on the summit of the towers remind us that this is indeed the brain and the heart of the Soviet world.

40

← 38, 39

42

41

43

45

46

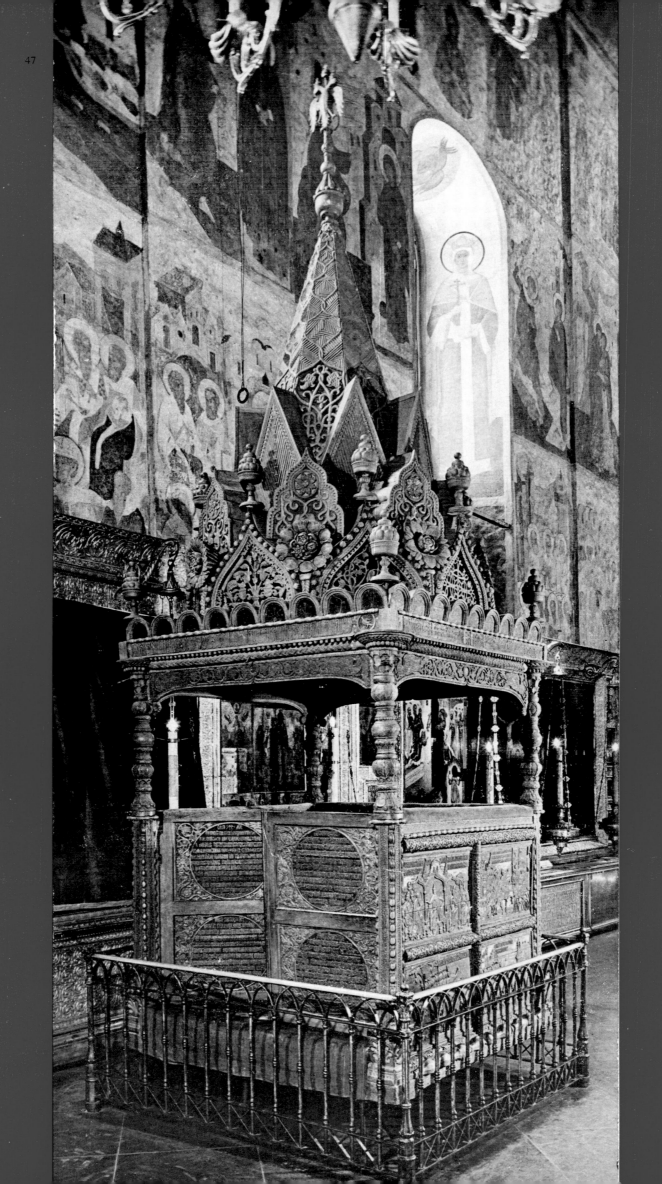

48

49

50, 51, 52, 53 →

55, 56→

58

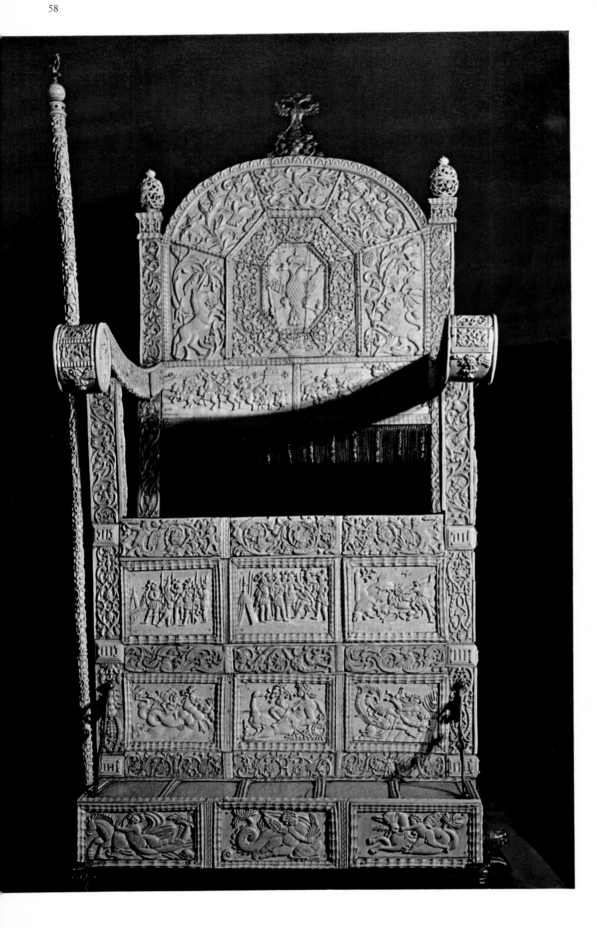

V THE ARBAT QUARTER

Those who want to see Russian life in its everyday reality, at its most ordinary and accessible level, must wander at random, paying no heed to where they are going, through the old streets of the Arbat quarter.

The minor nobility who lived here in former days are now represented by no more than a few street names, just as the old guilds of craftsmen are remembered in names which recall a long and picturesque past—the Street of the Trumpet-Players, the Street of the Curriers, the Street of the Old Stables, and so on. But their old wooden houses with the stucco facing are still occupied by characters who seem to have escaped from the pages of Chekhov or Gorky—clerks, students, artists, old workmen and good-natured old women. In summer all these honest citizens meet their friends in the parks to play chess amid the phlox and the pigeons.

62 *House at 4 Ostrovsky Street: timber faced with stucco.*

63 *House at 17 Kropotkin Street, once the property of Denis Davydov, a hero of the War of 1812.*

64 *Ostrovsky Street.*

65 *The last* izba *in Moscow.*

66 *The same: detail of carved woodwork round the windows.*

67 *Old private mansion at 24 Starokonyushnaya Street.*

68 *Pushkin Literary Museum, 12 Kropotkin Street. Built in 1814 by Domenico Gilardi, this house became in 1961 a museum of material on Pushkin's life in Moscow.*

69 *House of the boyar Saltykov (18th century), a fine example of the architecture of Russia in the feudal period.*

70–71 *Picturesque corners in the former Convent of the Conception (Zachatievsky).*

66

67

68

69

VI CONVENTS AND MONASTERIES

Once upon a time there were four hundred churches and religious houses in Moscow. Of these some two hundred are left—or about the same proportion as remained in Paris after the destructions carried out by Haussmann during the Second Empire.

The surviving churches, some still used for worship, some converted to other uses, have been restored—at any rate in Moscow—and are very carefully looked after. Their "heads" of gold or azure and the pink *shatyors* of their bell towers perpetuate the traditional image of the holy city which claimed to be the Third Rome.

The Novodevichy Convent is a magnificent complex of religious buildings. On its slopes, among the trees and the flowers, are the graves of some of the most illustrious sons of Russia—Gogol, Chekhov, Esenin, Mayakovsky, Prokofiev and Scriabin among them.

79

80

VII THE PUSHKIN MUSEUM

The museum which bears Pushkin's name owes nothing to the great Russian poet apart from the homage which is paid him and the example he gives of a poet receptive to all the cultures of Europe.

This splendid collection is mainly devoted to the arts of western Europe, and in particular to French painting and sculpture. Poussin and Renoir, Van Gogh and Cézanne, Rembrandt and Cranach all feel equally at home under the skies of Russia. The school-children and the soldiers who troop in their thousands through the museum every Sunday have long ceased to feel any surprise as they gaze at works by Matisse and Picasso. The Soviet people of today are well aware that these pictures have a meaning for them: they know that man does not live by bread alone.

←86

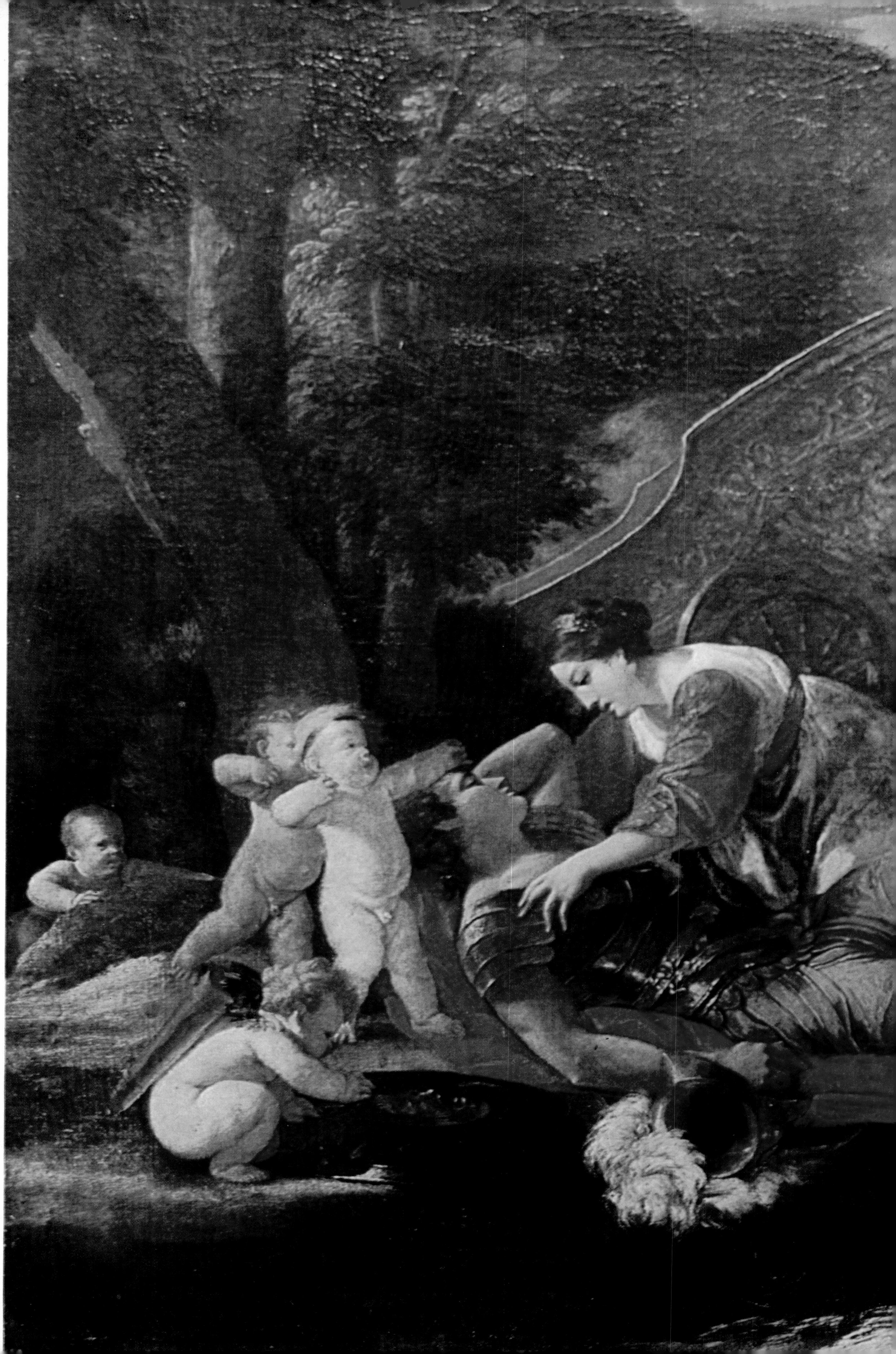

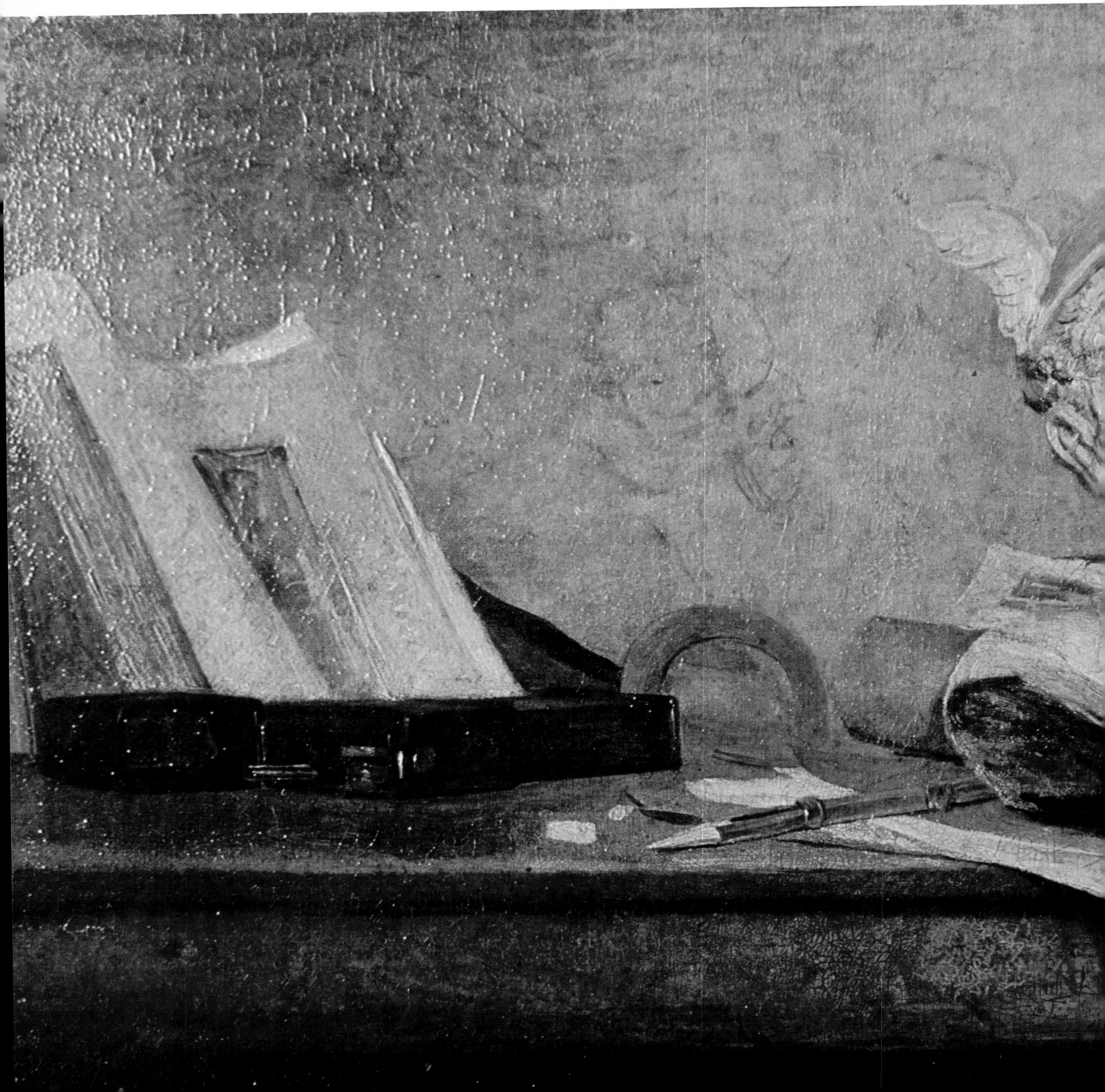

chardin

92

93

94

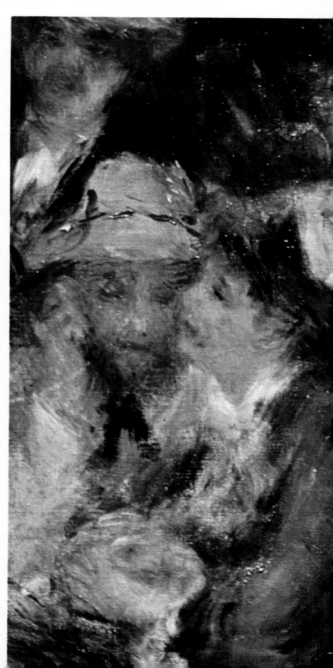

Degas

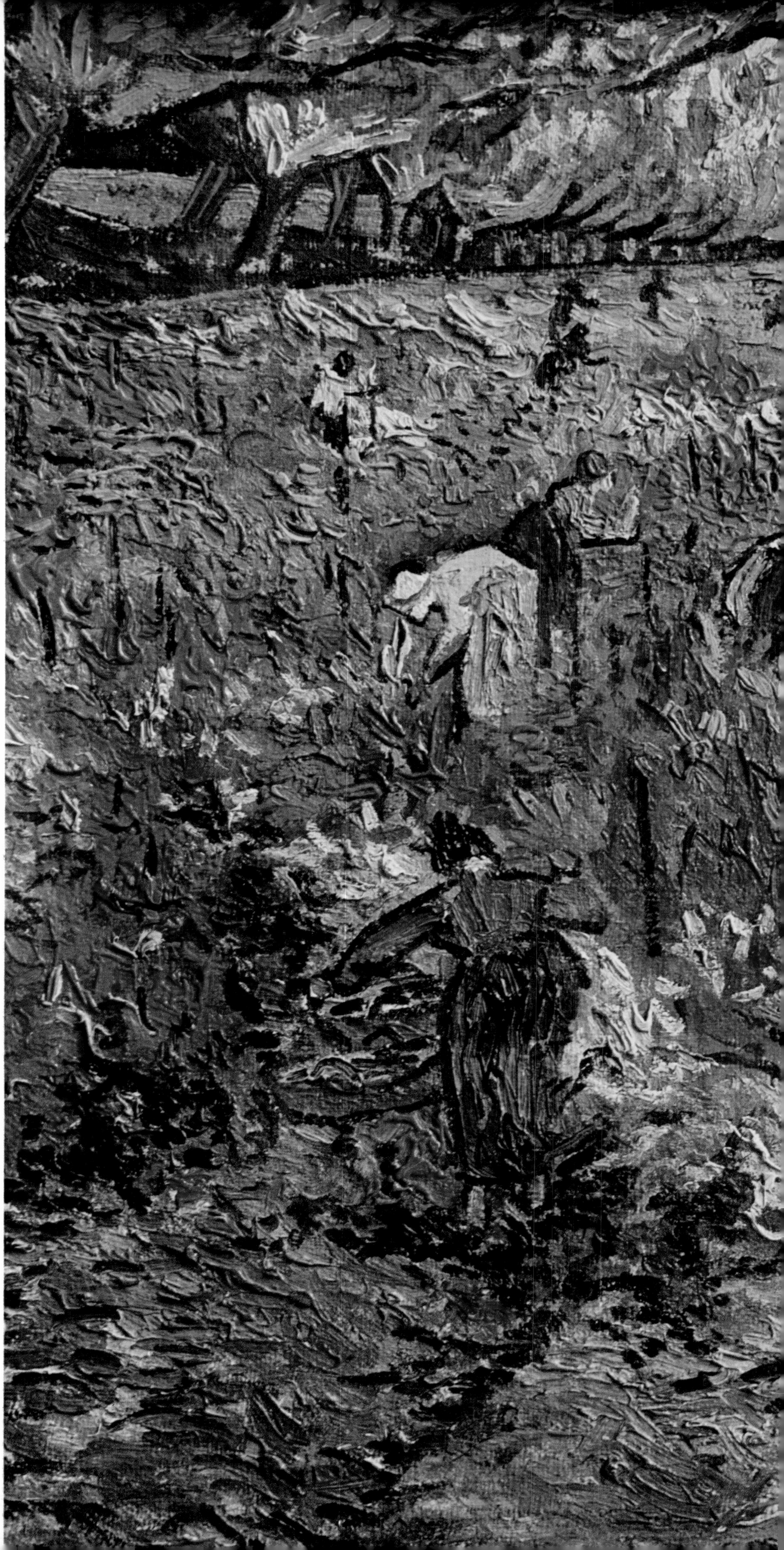

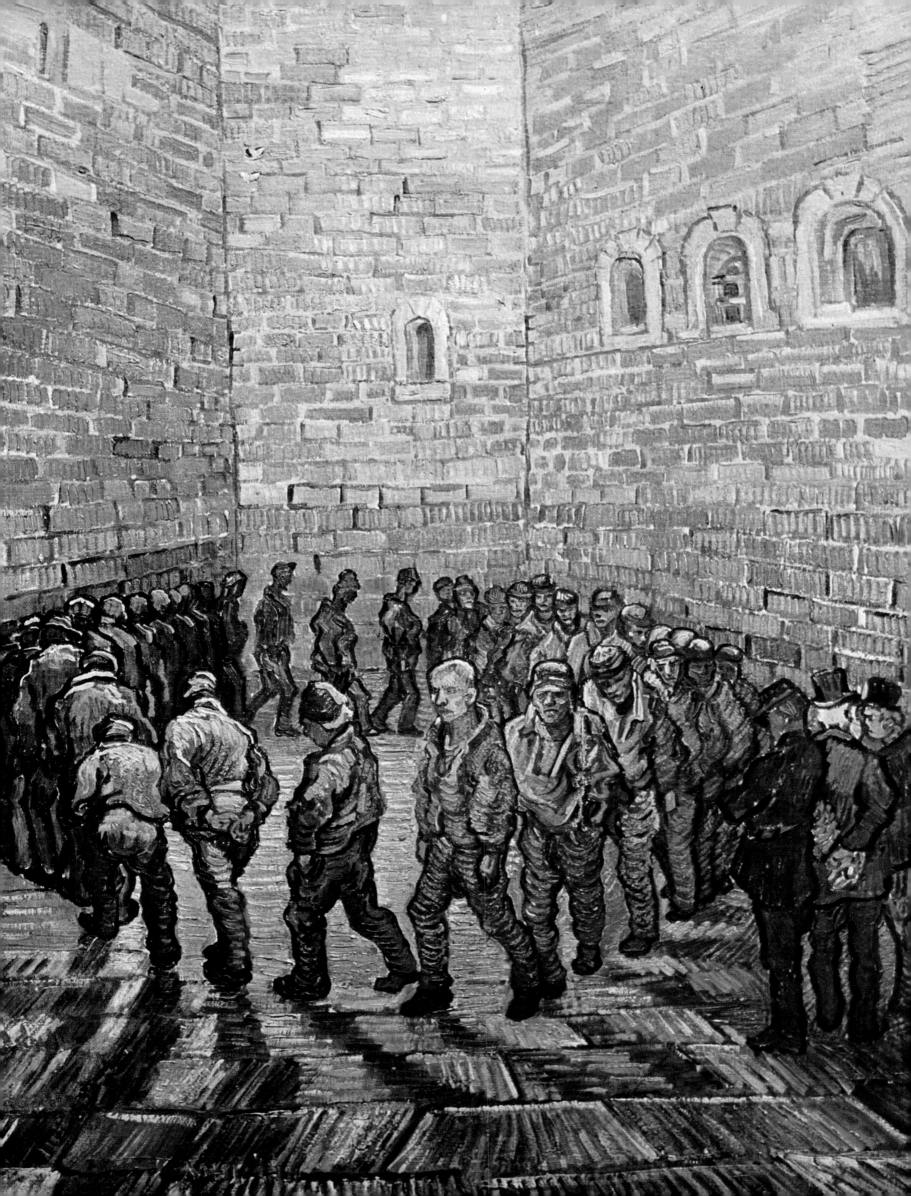

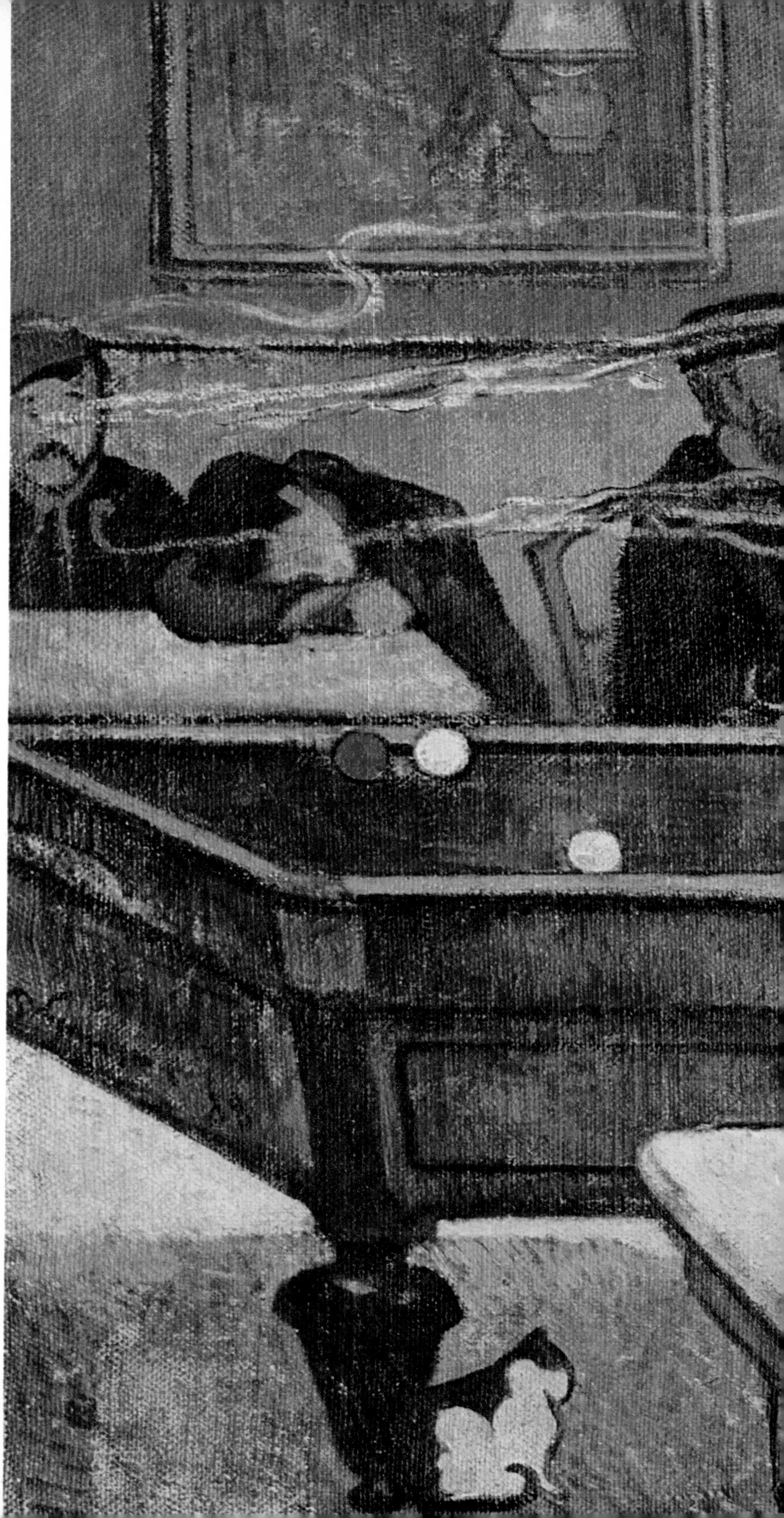

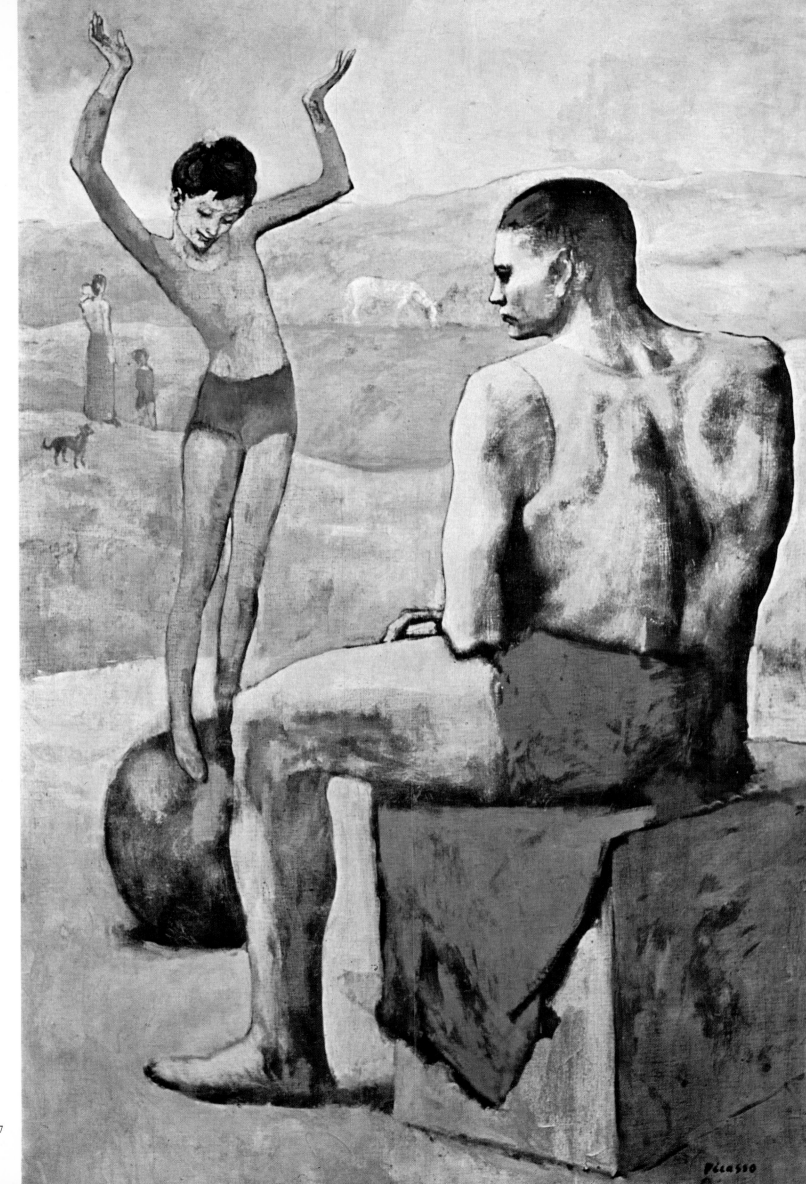

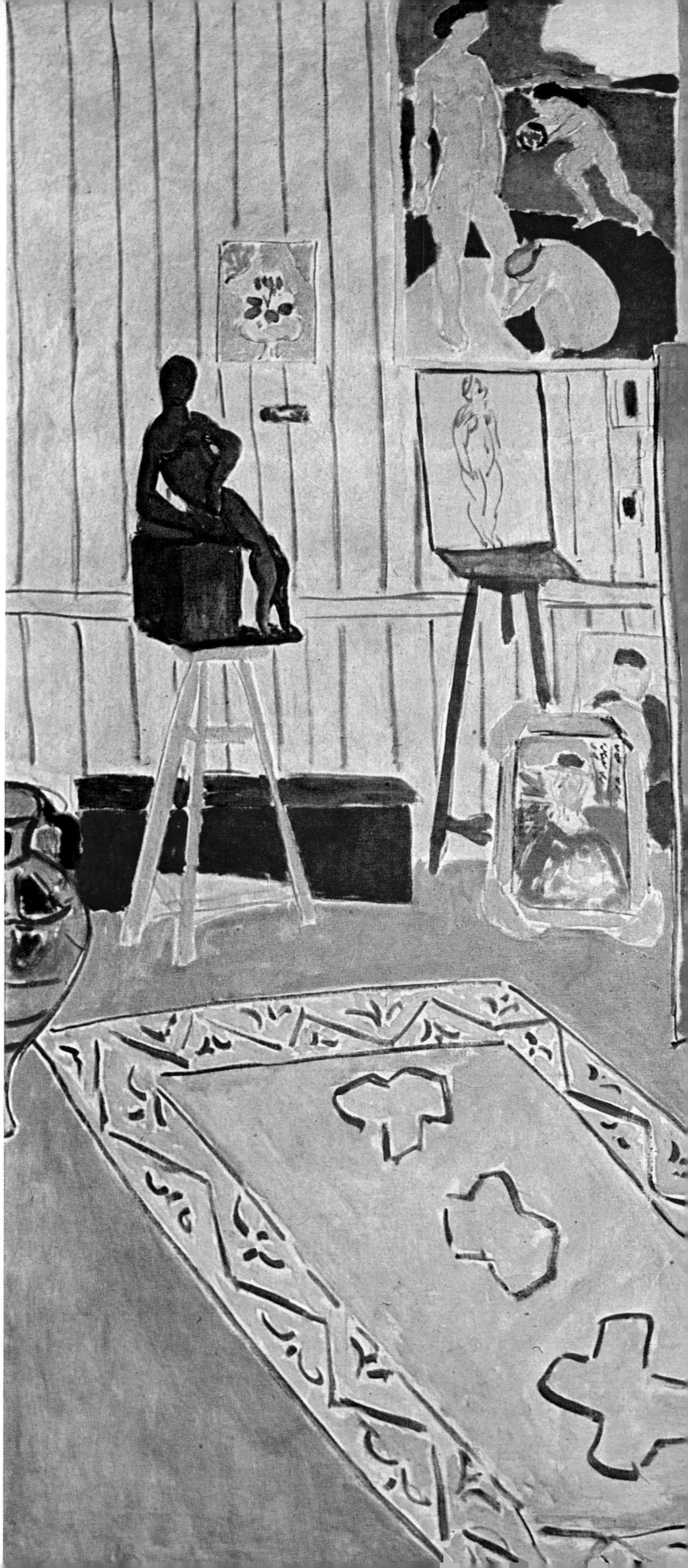

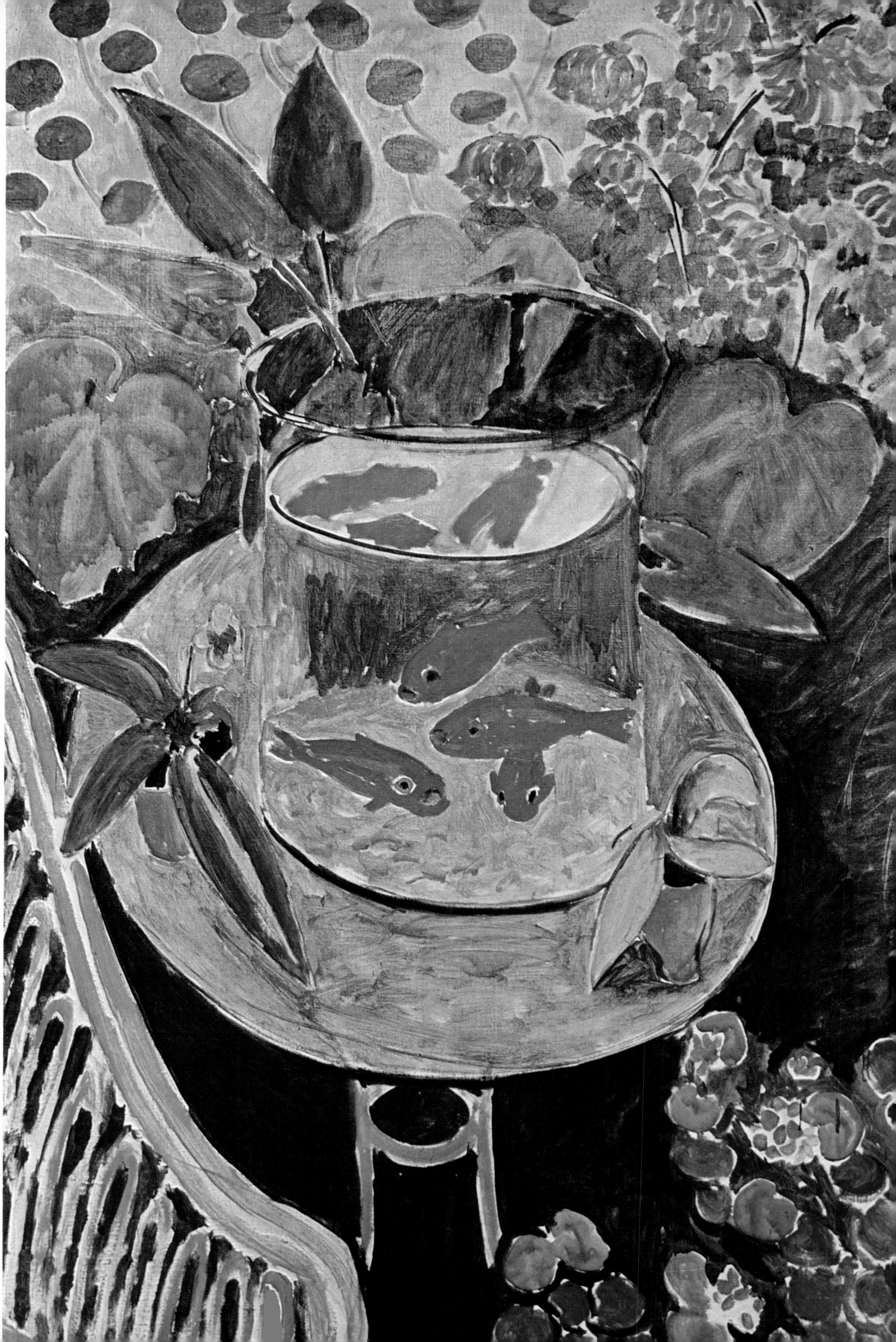

VIII THE TRETYAKOV GALLERY

The Tretyakov Gallery—that temple of Russian art—combines with the Russian Museum in Leningrad to display the best work of the painters and sculptors of Russia, from Rublev to the latest Soviet artists.

There is too much to see: the visitor who can afford only a single day may well feel discouraged. But those who persevere will discover all sorts of delights, dispersed unpredictably among huge and pretentious academic works—an unfamiliar study by Repin, a landscape by Levitan, a sketch by Ivanov or Vereshchagin, or some charming genre paintings, realistic and frequently satirical in tone, which have been overshadowed by showier and more popular works. When the new Tretyakov Gallery which is to be built on the banks of the river has provided more spacious accommodation for the display of all the twentieth century works now hidden away in store-rooms the world will be able to gain a fuller knowledge and appreciation of the distinctive genius of Russian art.

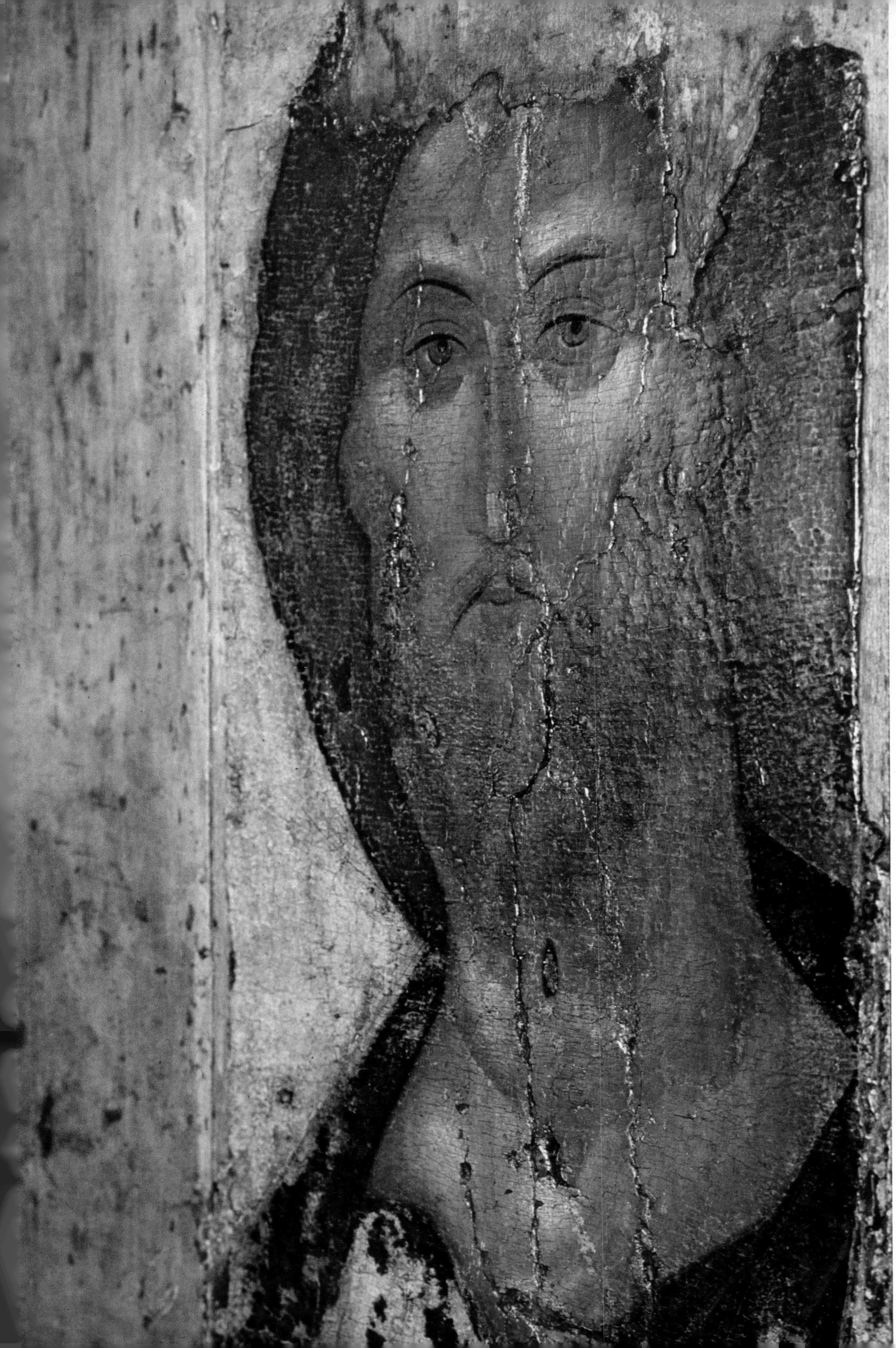

ЧЮДО СТГО ГЕWРГЫА WЗМИ

← 113

114

115

119

121

122

124

126

IX THE BORODINO PANORAMA

1812 was the year of the great invasion. Napoleon pressed his advance to the very heart of Russia, and Moscow was conquered, pillaged and burned.

At Borodino a huge circular building offers a panoramic reconstruction of one of the greatest battles in history. It was a contest between Russians and Frenchmen, between Kutuzov and Ney, between two opposing cavalries, between two armies of gallant soldiers. To the Russians it was the battle of Borodino, to the French the *bataille de la Moskova;* and both sides claimed the victory.

When the sun set on the evening of 7th September 90,000 dead were left on the field, Russians and Frenchmen fraternally intermingled. In wars of this kind there is no distinction between victors and vanquished: all are vanquished.

129

130

133

134

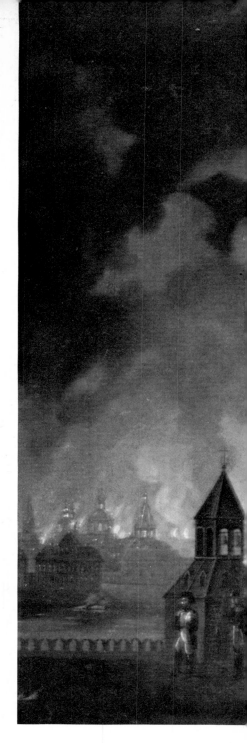

138

139

X THE STREETS AND SQUARES OF MOSCOW

What a pleasure it is to wander about Moscow on foot! The pavements are wide and shady; we can find refreshment at the booths of the ice-cream sellers, or potter round the open-air bookstalls; and there is always something of interest to watch. For those who do not mind using their legs there is so much to see on the "green boulevards", so many things and so many people to appeal to our curiosity, our sympathy or our sense of humour! The stations, the public buildings, the cafés, the statues of great men—all these offer an excuse for lingering, a stimulus to reverie, an opportunity to meet old friends and make new ones.

143

144

146

147

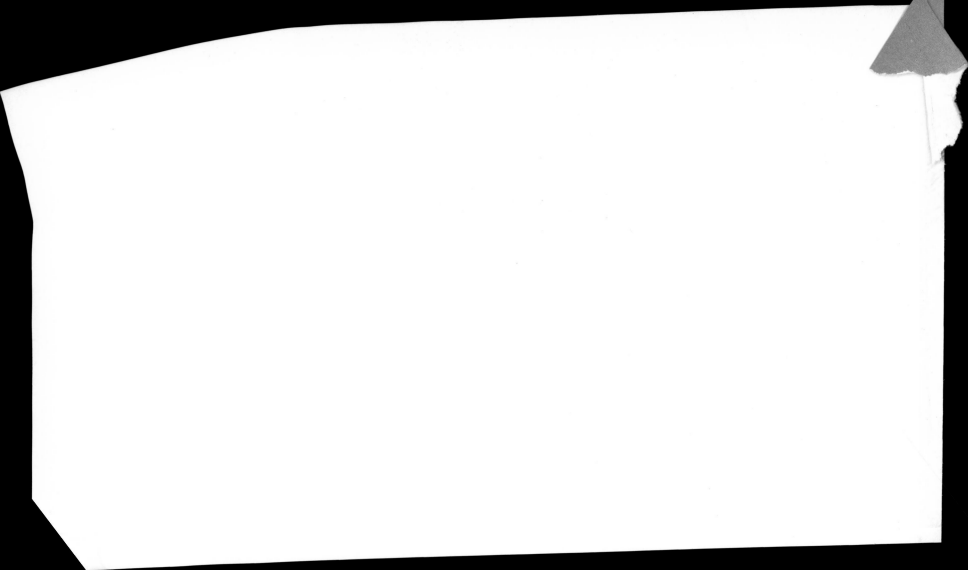

ВЕЛИКОМУ РУССКОМУ
КОМПОЗИТОРУ
ПЕТРУ ИЛЬИЧУ
ЧАЙКОВСКОМУ

153

154

155

156 →

XI ZAGORSK AND KOLOMENSKOYE

Zagorsk is a symphony in the baroque style, a concord of clangorous effects, a patchwork of many colours clustered round its ancient nucleus, the tomb of Saint Sergius, with its hidden jewel, the Church of the Holy Ghost, and a whole efflorescence of other churches, bell towers, palaces and miraculous fountains, constantly swarming with pilgrims and tourists.

Kolomenskoye is a pyramid soaring confidently heavenward, a spire which Berlioz compared with that of Strasbourg Cathedral, an old wooden bell tower rebuilt in stone, supported on a diadem-like pattern of arches, standing in pure and lonely beauty on a high platform three hundred feet above the Moskva. At its foot are the oaks planted by Peter the Great, the fortified tower brought from the distant north, and the great open plateau on which, under Eisenstein's direction, the knights of Ivan the Terrible fought their battle once again. In winter not a soul is to be seen here; and in the cemetery on the hill, a few hundred yards away, the dead sleep under the snow.

157 *Zagorsk: the campanile. Height 290 feet; designed by Rastrelli and built by Prince Ukhtomsky between 1741 and 1767.*

158 *Zagorsk: general view of the Monastery of the Trinity and St Sergius.*

159 *Zagorsk: the entrance porch on the left, with a baroque tower on the right.*

160 *Zagorsk: tomb of St Sergius, who founded the monastery in 1340.*

161 *Zagorsk: Church of the Trinity, built in 1422.*

162 *Zagorsk: Chapel of the Miraculous Fountain.*

163 *Zagorsk: tomb of Boris Godunov's family.*

164 *Zagorsk: Church of the Holy Ghost, built in 1554.*

165 *Zagorsk: icon in mosaic work in the Cathedral of the Dormition. Virgin and Child. 18th century.*

166 *Zagorsk: 18th century baroque palace, used as a residence by the Patriarch of Moscow when visiting the monastery.*

167 *Kolomenskoye: fortified wooden tower, of the type which developed into the* shatyor *(tower of pyramidal shape — cf. Plate 170).*

168 *Wood-carving: an example of the work produced by local craftsmen. Zagorsk Museum.*

169 *Kolomenskoye: Church of Our Lady of Kazan. 17th century.*

170 *Kolomenskoye: Church of the Ascension. Built in 1533 and restored in 1880, this is the finest example in Russia of a church with a pyramidal tower.*

160

159

XII THE PALACES

The countryside round Moscow was a popular resort of the nobility in the eighteenth and nineteenth centuries, when a period of assured peace made it possible to live there in ease and security. Like other countries in Europe, Russia was covered with a rash of small-scale copies of Versailles. They were designed by architects brought from abroad, but they were built by Russian builders—often, indeed, by serfs, who showed supreme skill in adapting the local building material, timber, to the patterns of classical architecture.

These attractive and rather melancholy mansions have now taken a fresh lease of life as museums or rest homes. With their tall white walls, their *trompe-l'œil* colonnades, their belvederes and their French-style gardens, they blend perfectly into the magnificent harmony and serenity of the countryside round Moscow.

184

185

186

187

188

189

194

196

195

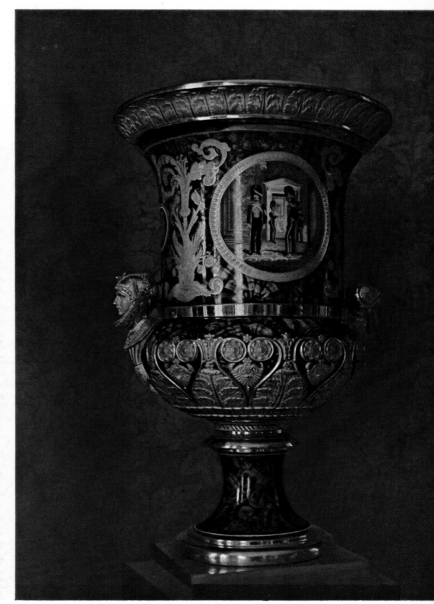

197

198→

XIII YASNAYA POLYANA

There is no more fascinating shrine than the estate on which Tolstoy was born, where he spent the greater part of his restless life, and where at last he found repose under a nameless grassy mound. Here, for four score years, his genius grew and matured, proclaiming and developing the humanitarian ideals of his century.

Passing through the rooms of the house, we follow the life of this great man from birth to death. We see his library, the books which he used to read and annotate. We see his work-table, his bed. We share his inmost thoughts and feelings—tormented as they often were—and those of his wife Sofya Andreevna. We accompany him on his walks in the park, through the woods in which as a child he sought the "green stick", the key to universal love and happiness.

We read Yasnaya Polyana as we read a book; for Tolstoy put it all into his books. We recognise the places he describes and people them with the characters of his novels, the real inhabitants of this house and estate. The perishable substance of human life is transformed by his genius into a pattern of immortal myths, a fabric of ideas, a creation of the spirit.

199 *Tolstoy's grave, in a leafy corner of the park.*

200 *Tolstoy's house, in which he lived from 1862 to 1910.*

201 *The "poor folk's tree", where Tolstoy liked to meet the ordinary people of the district.*

202 *Tolstoy's library. (Ph. J.-P. Gaume).*

203 *Tolstoy's old Remington typewriter. (Ph. J.-P. Gaume).*

204 *Tolstoy's bedroom. (Ph. J.-P. Gaume).*

205 *The kitchens.*

206 *Kramskoy (1837–1887): Portrait of Tolstoy. Tretyakov Gallery.*

207 *Corrected proofs of Tolstoy's* Resurrection. *(Ph. Novosti).*

208 *A page from the manuscript of the second draft of* War and Peace. *At the foot of the page Tolstoy has drawn a plan of the positions of the armies at the battle of Borodino. (Ph. Novosti).*

209 *Drawing of a horse by Tolstoy, dated 3rd December 1909. (Ph. Novosti).*

210 *A page from the manuscript of* Anna Karenina. *(Ph. Novosti).*

211 *The* izba *of Tolstoy's coachman.*

212 *Tolstoy's favourite walk in the park.*

213 *One of the many lakes in the park of Yasnaya Polyana. (Ph. J.-P. Gaume).*

203

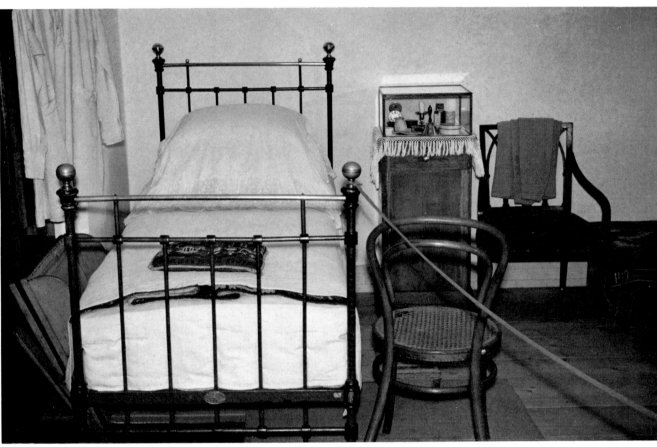

204

205

202

206

207

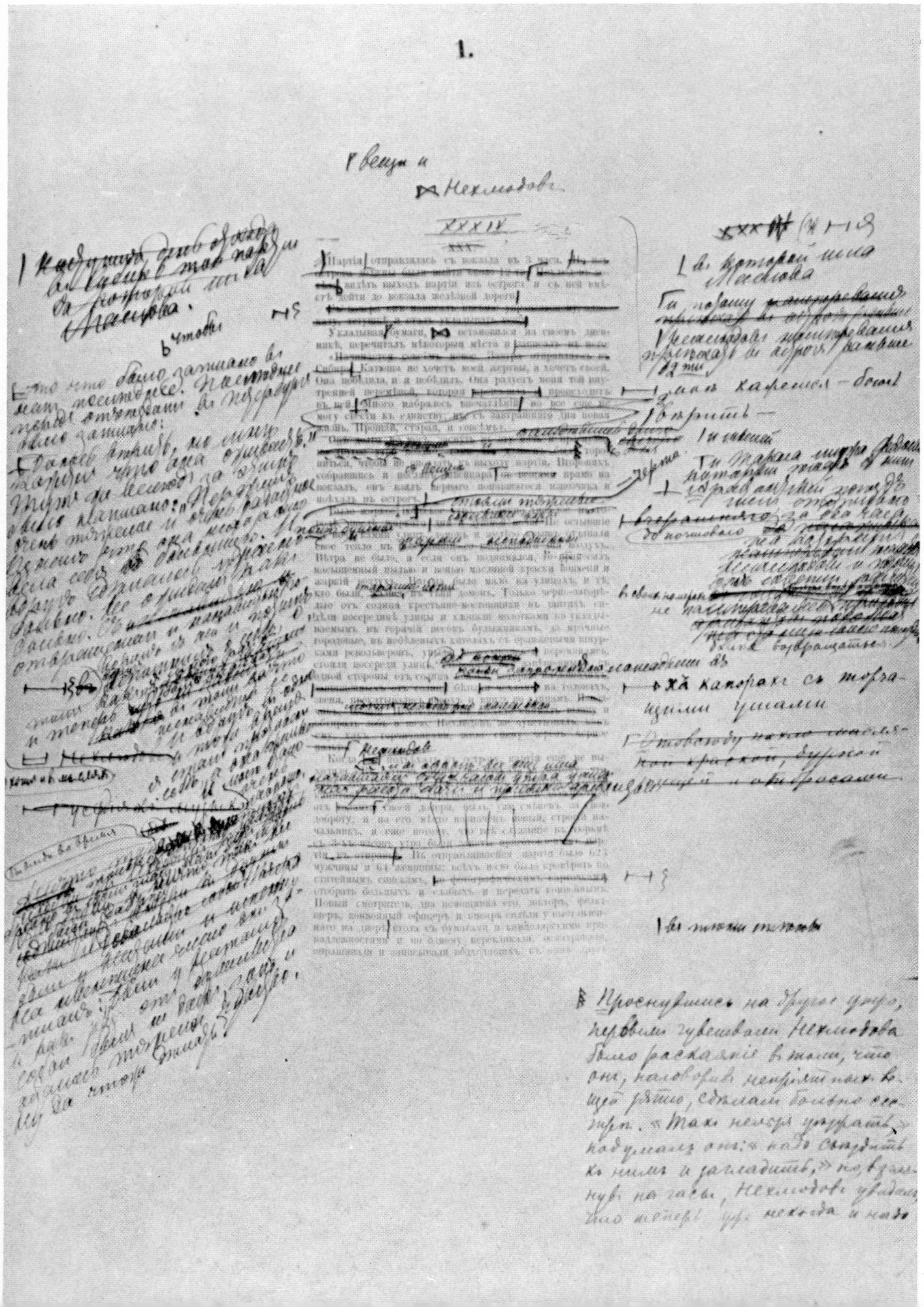

1.

XXXIV

Проснувшись на другое утро, первымъ чувствомъ Нехлюдова было раскаяніе въ томъ, что онъ, наговоривъ непріятныхъ вещей зятю, сдѣлалъ больно сестрѣ. «Такъ нельзя уѣзжать, — подумалъ онъ, — надо съѣздить къ нимъ и загладить». Но, взглянувъ на часы, Нехлюдовъ увидалъ, что теперь уже некогда и надо

208

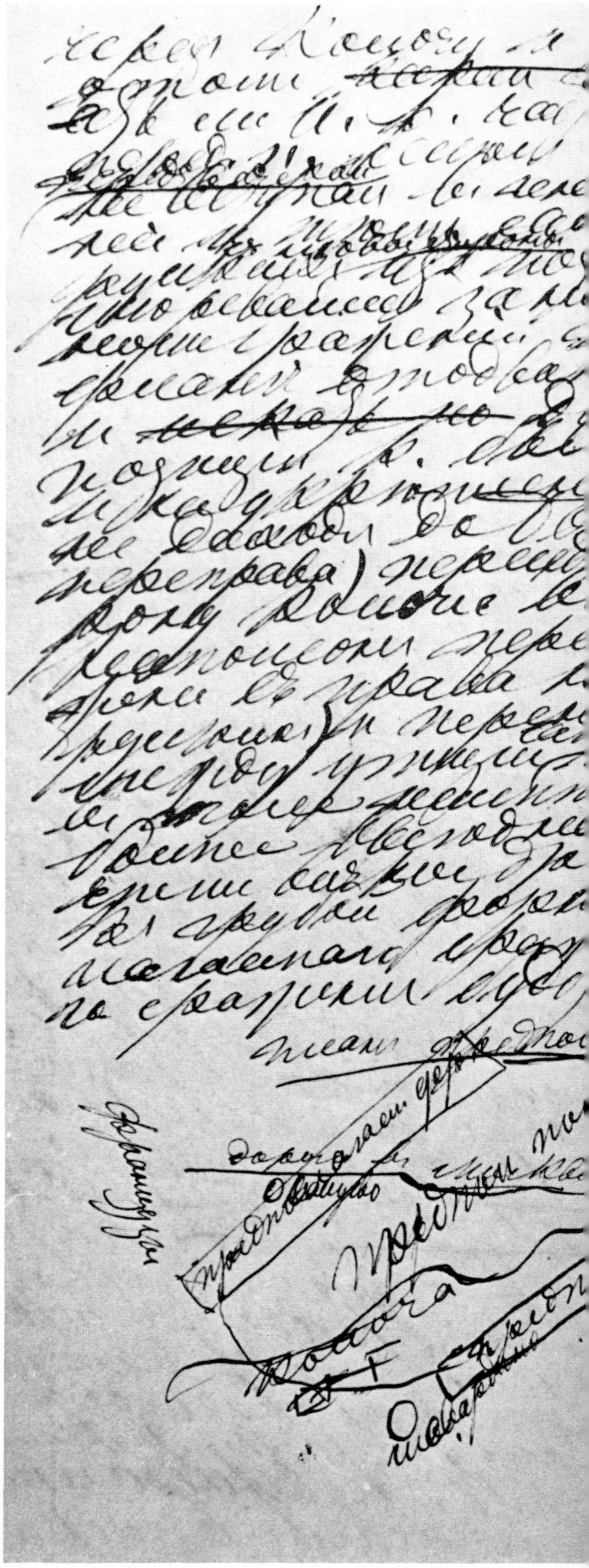

209

210

Нарисовал Л. Н. Толстой 3. дек. 1909

211

212

213

XIV LENINSKIE GORKI

Lenin loved this charming neo-classical mansion built in the heart of the countryside by the whim of a military governor of bygone days; but he thought little of the architecture or the furnishings of the house. He and his wife, the faithful Nadezhda Konstantinovna Krupskaya, lived here very simply, using only one or two rooms filled with the familiar objects they brought back from exile, in which they liked to receive their old revolutionary comrades. When Lenin was completely immobilised by illness it was from here, linked to the Kremlin by telephone, that he pressed on with the forging of the new Soviet state—until at last, on 21st January 1924, he died on his iron bedstead, surrounded by peasants.

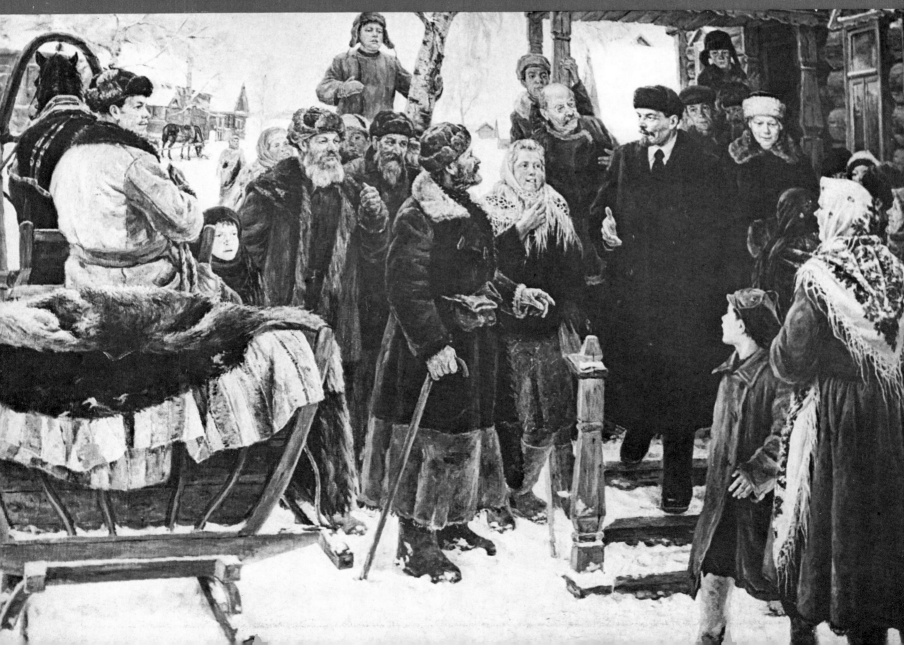

221

222

224

225

XV MAY DAY

First thought of in the United States, and then taken over by the socialist militants of Europe, the 1st of May has become the triumphant festival of the workers of the Soviet Union. The military parade and the march-past of sportsmen are of less significance than the great demonstration by the people of Moscow, who all day long file through Red Square singing their national songs, full of gay and confident strength. On this spring day they feel the truth of the poet's remark—"man's future is in man".

231

232

XVI ENTERTAINMENTS

The Russians have always been fond of public spectacles and entertainments. They are born actors, excelling in the drama, in dancing, music, the cinema and all the collective arts. Political congresses are also a form of celebration, and the same buildings serve both purposes. In Russia we find huge theatres, well equipped stages, carefully trained companies, responsive and enthusiastic audiences, a close communion between actors and spectators, the subordination of each individual to the group, and of all of them to the art or the idea which transcends them. We must go to the Bolshoi Theatre, the Palace of Congresses, or the Tchaikovsky Conservatoire if we want to appreciate fully the fervour and power of the Russian soul, united in a sense of community.

260→

LIST OF ILLUSTRATIONS

Front end-paper: *General view of the Kitay-Gorod in the 17th century. Detail from a plan of Moscow of 1638. (Ph. Novosti).*

Back end-paper: *Plan of the Kremlin from the Beled Album (1600-1605). State Historical Museum. (Ph. Novosti).*

Except where otherwise indicated, all the photographs were taken by Gérard Bertin, Geneva.

PRINTED IN SWITZERLAND

CONTENTS

PRINTED IN JULY 1967 ON THE PRESSES OF NAGEL PUBLISHERS, GENEVA

THE BINDING WAS EXECUTED IN THE WORKSHOPS OF NAGEL PUBLISHERS, GENEVA

PLATES IN BLACK AND WHITE AND COLOUR ENGRAVED BY CLICHÉS UNION, PARIS

THE PUBLISHER'S LEGAL DEPOSIT NUMBER IS 430

PRINTED IN SWITZERLAND

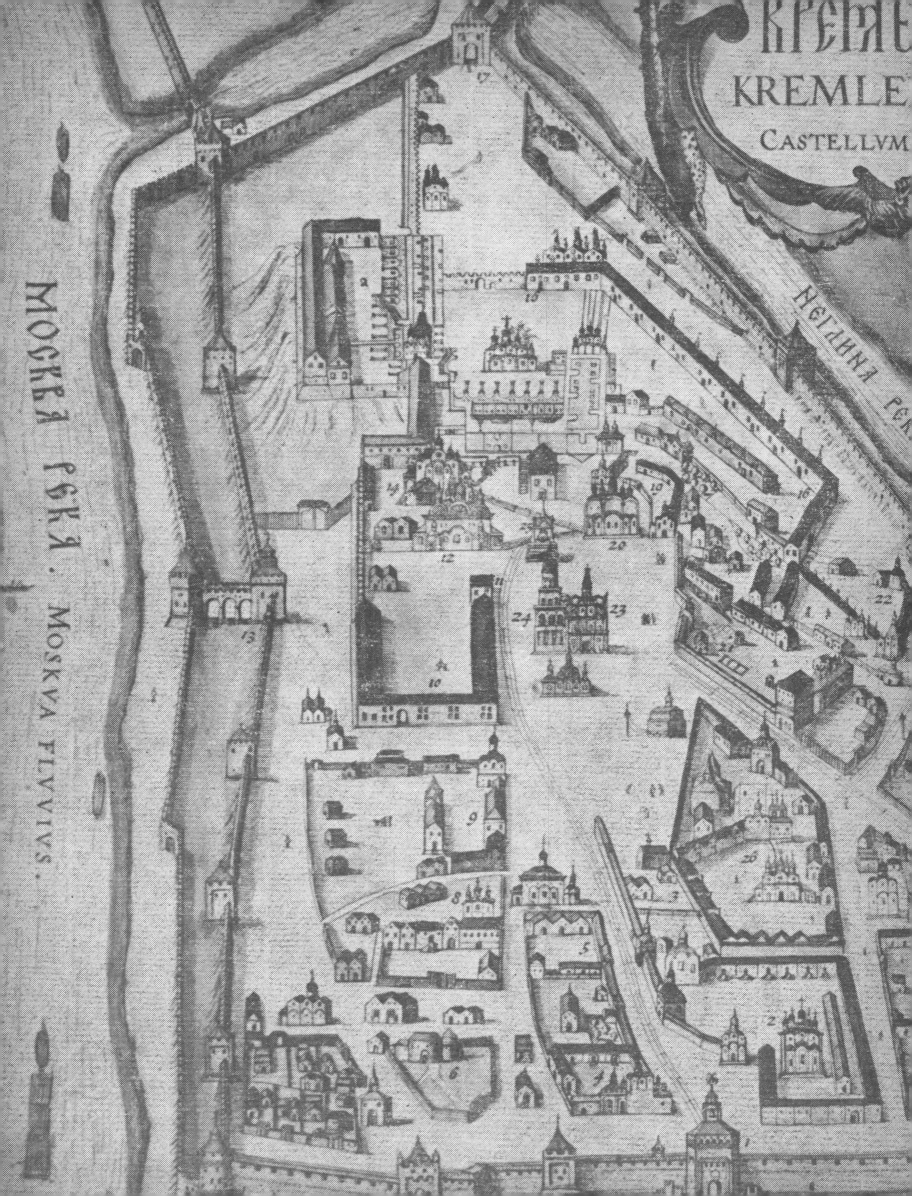

КРЕМ
KREMLE
CASTELLVM

NEGLINNA RE

МОСКВА РѢКА. MOSKVA FLVVIVS.